Immaterial

a collection of compositions

Jason Thomas

ISBN 978-0-578-15481-7

10th ANNIVERSARY EDITION

DEATH-SPIRAL

0,2

LOS ANGELES 2014

Foreword: Ten Years Later

Ten years ago I finished the collection of compositions entitled *Immaterial*. This work was my attempt to create something that would demonstrate the ideas of *subject music* through actual pieces rather than explanatory text. At the time the pieces were written (2002-2004) I had composed a limited number of pieces in the instrumental and computer music idioms, finding both situations less than appealing for different reasons. Writing for instruments too often involved the expectation that one would attempt to exploit the characteristics of the instrument itself, making the idea subservient to the tool supposedly employed for its implementation. Those working in the electronic and computer idiom similarly shared the same fetish-like obsession with devices, evidencing this interest with several works intending to document their process of realization in the same way that experimental composers of a past generation made pieces that documented the composition process. In addition to this technology focus, I found myself forced to address issues that were of minute relevance, akin to asking a playwright not only to select specific costumes, but sew them himself. My solution to this dilemma was the process of composition I call *subject music*, the practical and philosophical aspects of which I will address.

The practical techniques of subject music can be employed in any style or genre of composition. This simply involves stating the perceptual results desired rather than the physical acts to be performed upon an object, as is the case with most notations in a traditional score. As a variety of technologies make themselves available and are utilized for musical purposes, it is less likely that a single set of tools may be considered standard (as has been the case with traditional instrumental configurations), nor is it evident that such standardization is even desired. The wishes of a composer as stated in such a work may in fact be better realized by a tool that is not currently known to the composer, or does not even yet exist. More important than this, however, is the fact that even if all indicated physical acts are performed, the desired perceptual result may not occur. The process of composing subject music allows for any means of accomplishing a desired result, rather than asking simply that the right buttons be pressed at the right time.

From a philosophical standpoint, one must, if writing a piece or creating any other work requiring the participation of others, ask oneself what would constitute a successful realization or interpretation. Recognizing that no work is guaranteed to receive a successful realization at all times or even frequently, I consider that such a success occurs (via traditional instruments, computer technology or any other means, including imagination only) when the desired perceptual features are effectively perceived, not simply when a specific series of physical actions is completed as directed, regardless of how accurately this is done. In most instances, I avoid stating instructions in terms of physical actions entirely.

Not surprisingly, a change in method of composition necessitates a change in performance practice. In the case of subject music, many pieces are unlikely to achieve their best interpretation through a physical performance at all. In *Immaterial*, all pieces are to be imagined—an opportune method owing to the brief and simple nature of the works. The attention span of most listeners renders imaginary realization generally practical only for short pieces, the instructions of which may be carried out without reference during the process of imagining. Longer or more complex works are generally best realized via live performance or electronic playback, although the decision is best made by those who actually carry out the performance or other realization of the piece. Most of my scores not intended for imaginary realization use general instructions that allow those reading the score a great degree of flexibility to utilize whatever tools to accomplish the desired perceptual results, either in performance, technological production intended for subsequent playback, or a combination of the two.

Less obvious than the physical presence of a performing ensemble is the physical nature of the desired response to a given work within the listener. Others have referred to "body genres" in film and literature, for example. Suspense as well as comedic and erotic aspects all focus not only on the physicality of presentation but also on the physical response of the perceiver. I have attempted to remove this aspect from my own works, recognizing that doing otherwise would result only in a novel process in service of a similar end, not a difference of substance.

Many of the pieces in *Immaterial* were initially distributed electronically or in programs accompanying a live performance of other works, received by a small group of individuals familiar with my efforts in this area. The first copy of the full collection was given to composer Mark So, who incidentally noticed several errors in grammar, inconsistencies in the usage of specific terms, formatting irregularities and other general errors that would likely have made such an initial draft unnecessarily confusing for many readers. I am extremely thankful for his assistance in completing a long overdue presentation of these pieces.

In the short span of history since the completion of *Immaterial*, the ideas exemplified by the works do not appear novel at all. An entire subsequent generation is just as likely to have had as their introduction to creative music-making the general sound source of the computer as any physical instrument. While it is easy to focus on the practical implications of this development, it is the change in philosophy and methodology that is most important.

From a personal standpoint, I am relieved to finally present, ten years following completion, a work that clearly exemplifies the ideas that I have implemented since 2002, and attempted to philosophically reconcile into a consistent practice beforehand. In the last several years my personal time has unfortunately been divided among several business ventures unrelated to composition, leaving the completion, documentation and presentation of my works with inadequate attention, a situation I will likely continually struggle to rectify.

My early questions as a composer revolved around our need to categorize our musical experiences by physical rather than perceptual traits. Why did three leading conservatories not allow applications from those with my principal performance instrument (the saxophone) in the mid 90s? Why did the large chain record store I patronized in Boston and New York place a release of the orchestral arrangements of a well-known pop musician in the "classical" section, despite exhibiting no substantive change to the pieces other than instrumentation?

I knew such viewpoints were misguided but had not yet formed a practical alternative for my own works. Now, in less than twenty years, a few things have changed. The above conservatories have all reversed their previous position regarding the training of composers relative to their choice of instrument, and the record chain in question no longer exists. I expect the idea of what it is to be a musician in general to change substantially going forward, becoming to an even greater degree decoupled from the sources that are used to produce sound. It would actually please me if the limited number of individuals who become aware of this work approached it with indifference, taking such pieces to represent nothing more than a demonstration of the blatantly obvious.

Jason Thomas, Autumn 2014

Immaterial

Main Entry: **im·ma·te·ri·al**
Pronunciation: \ˌi-mə-ˈtir-ē-əl\
Function: *adjective*
Etymology: Middle English *immaterial,* from Late Latin *immaterialis,* from Latin *in-* + Late Latin *materialis* material
1 : not consisting of matter : INCORPOREAL
2 : of no substantial consequence : UNIMPORTANT

Merriam-Webster

The analysis of our sensations when it cannot be attached to corresponding differences in external objects, meets with peculiar difficulties, the nature and significance of which will have to be considered hereafter. The attention of the observer has generally to be drawn to the phenomenon he has to observe, by peculiar aids properly selected, until he knows precisely what to look for; after he has once succeeded, he will be able to throw aside such crutches.

Hermann von Helmholtz

Do you think that when the spirit comes to me I consider your lousy fiddles?

Ludwig van Beethoven

Ibid?

These works may be experienced in various ways. Initially, many individual pieces were placed on stands in a concert setting or posted on the internet. Within a few parameters, the works may be presented in many ways, although I caution against two possible realizations: reading the texts aloud or projecting individual lines sequentially to a screen. The former is problematic due to the potential for one's voice to interfere with the imaginary sounds, while the latter forces the reader to follow a specific pace, an undesirable restriction for these specific works. Ultimately, the preferred method of realization is to memorize the concept of the piece, reading it beforehand and then imagining the piece in its entirety without the intrusion of cumbersome text.

These works exist as perceived; they are not this bound volume.

Immaterial

for anyone, if it matters

imagine a sound with no physical source

More of the Same

for anyone, as long as they wish

imagine a sound

attempt to imagine the sound exactly as before

Less of the Same

for anyone up for a change

imagine a sound

imagine a sound differing in as many aspects as possible

Assemblies I

for anyone

each of the following lines contains characteristics of a single sound to be imagined

long loud pitched

long soft pitched

long loud unpitched

long soft unpitched

short loud pitched

short soft pitched

short loud unpitched

short soft unpitched

Assemblies II

for anyone

each of the following lines contains characteristics of a single sound to be imagined

abruptly beginning, steadily sustaining for some time, gradually ending

gradually beginning, steadily sustaining for some time, abruptly ending

gradually beginning, steadily sustaining for some time, gradually ending

abruptly beginning, steadily sustaining for some time, abruptly ending

Assemblies III

for anyone

each of the following lines contains characteristics of a single sound to be imagined

static amplitude, static frequency, static timbre

changing amplitude, static frequency, static timbre

static amplitude, changing frequency, static timbre

static amplitude, static frequency, changing timbre

static amplitude, changing frequency, changing timbre

changing amplitude, static frequency, changing timbre

changing amplitude, changing frequency, static timbre

changing amplitude, changing frequency, changing timbre

Change In

for anyone

imagine a sustaining sound comprised of several component parts repeating in rapid succession to result in the perception of a single texture

gradually imagine the succession decreasing in rapidity until eventually each individual component sound can be perceived

continue to imagine this succession of sounds in a motoric rhythmic pattern

gradually imagine the succession of sounds increasing in rapidity until a single texture is again perceived

Switch Piece

for anyone

simultaneously imagine two sustaining sounds

vary your focus from one to the other

Through Piece

for anyone

imagine a sound

imagine the same sound, almost entirely obstructed by a mass of other sounds

imagine the sound again, unobstructed

Periodicity

for anyone

imagine a periodic sound perceived as having pitch

imagine the same pitch repeatedly, each time with a different timbral quality

Sets

for anyone

imagine a series of sounds, all occurring sequentially, perceived as a single group

imagine the same series of sounds occurring in such a way that internal subgroupings are perceived

continue to imagine various subgroupings until the possibilities of the sequence are exhausted

imagine each member of the series so that the sounds are perceived individually

Offsets

for anyone

imagine two sounds of similar timbre beginning at the same time

imagine the same two sounds, one beginning slightly later

imagine the sounds with an increased offset in start time until they occur in sequence

Continuity

for anyone

choose some parameter of sound that is variable in a continuous manner

imagine a sound beginning at the lower extreme of this parameter and proceeding over some period of time to the upper extreme

without pause, imagine the sound decreasing from the upper extreme of this parameter back to the lower extreme

to the extent possible, attempt not to allow other aspects of the sound to change in response to the parameter you have chosen

Discretion

for anyone

imagine a sound changing continuously (without steps) in one parameter from some point to another

imagine the same sound changing in the same parameter by the same amount, but this time by step, not passing through all possible values but changing at some consistent interval

continue to imagine the sound with an increased step size for the amount of change, until you eventually imagine the sound only at an initial and final state

Indiscretion

for anyone

imagine a continual bed of sound, inactive in nature, at a low volume

with no regular pattern, imagine from time to time a short sound of extremely high volume

continue to imagine the bed of sound undisturbed and unaltered

Modulations

for anyone

imagine a sustaining sound having pitch, continually varying in the following parameters

volume

pitch

timbre

volume and pitch

pitch and timbre

volume and timbre

volume, pitch, and timbre

Difference

for anyone

imagine a sustaining sound, variable in some aspect

imagine the sound varying in this parameter the least possible amount over time

imagine the sound varying in this parameter the greatest possible amount over time

imagine two simultaneous versions of the sound, varying the smallest possible amount from one another in the chosen parameter

imagine two simultaneous versions of the sound, varying the greatest possible amount from one another in the chosen parameter

imagine the sound alone again, as before

Sieves

for anyone, or any group (with some exclusions, of course...)

imagine a mass of several sounds

continue to imagine a mass of sounds, excluding those containing some particular characteristic

continue with a different characteristic as many times as desired

imagine the initial sound mass as before

Transformation I (Discrete)

for anyone

imagine the same sound repeated a number of times

imagine the sound the same number of times, each instance varying in some aspect

imagine the sound the same number of times, varying in several aspects

imagine a new sound the same number of times

Transformation II (Continuous)

for anyone

imagine a sound

imagine another sound, varying in some way

imagine a gradual change over time from one to the other

Primacy

for anyone

imagine a particular sequence of sounds, the first of which is perceived as having primary significance

imagine the same sequence of sounds, the second of which is perceived as having primary significance

continue this process with a varying number of sounds in sequence and various means by which super- and sub-ordinate status is established (rhythmic displacement, volume, etc.)

Elision

for anyone

imagine a series of sounds perceived as a group

imagine a second series of sounds also perceived as a group

imagine one group after the other, elided

Groups I

for anyone

imagine a group of sounds, dissimilar in nature though occurring sequentially with no pause between

Groups II

for anyone

imagine a sequence of sounds, similar in timbre though separated by silence

Groups III

for anyone

imagine a group of several sounds, changing randomly in some parameter

imagine a subgroup of several sounds within the first group, changing in the same way while the remaining sounds continue to change at random

Just Noticeable

for anyone listening closely

imagine a sound

imagine a sound differing by the smallest perceptible amount in some aspect

Limit

for anyone, up to a point

imagine two simultaneous sounds differing by the smallest possible amount in some aspect

Extremities

for anyone

imagine a sound that is extreme in some parameter

imagine the opposite extremity in this parameter

Moderation

for anyone

imagine a sound exhibiting no extremity in any parameter

Pulse I

for anyone

imagine a sound repeated at a regular time interval so that a rhythmic pulse is established

gradually over time vary the sound used to establish the pulse until each time a different sound is used

gradually return to the exclusive use of the initial sound

Pulse II

for anyone

imagine a series of sounds establishing a specific rhythmic pulse

simultaneously imagine another series of sounds with no discernible rhythmic pulse

Pulse III

for anyone

imagine a sustaining sound, varying in some parameter at a regular interval of time

From Rubato

for anyone

imagine a strict rhythmic pattern continually repeated

gradually imagine greater degrees of variation within individual rhythmic units, distributing duration from one unit to that preceding or following it while maintaining the overall sense of pulse

continue to vary the rhythmic units until a single rhythmic pulse can no longer be perceived

Viewpoints

for anyone

*imagine a sound followed by silence, so much that the next sonic event is perceived not as a
member of a group with the first, but independently*

*imagine the sound again, followed by a little less silence, then continue with decreasing lengths
of silence in between until each sound is no longer perceived as an independent event alone but
also as a member of a series*

*continue to increase the speed of successive sound events until no silence intervenes and there is
no discernible difference between the sounds, perceived as a single sustaining sound*

*reverse the process until you again perceive individual sounds separated by silence and
perceived independently*

Line Obstruction

for anyone

imagine two simultaneous low volume sounds

gradually imagine one sound increasing in volume until the other sound is no longer heard

Contour Paths

for anyone

imagine a single static sound

imagine a single sound changing over time from one extreme in any parameter to the opposite extreme in the same parameter

imagine a series of sounds one after another, starting at one extreme of a particular parameter and gradually approaching the opposite extreme in the same parameter

imagine a series of sounds, all of which are the same

Breakpoints

for anyone

imagine a sustaining sound changing from one point to another in a particular parameter over the entire duration of the sound

imagine another sustaining sound changing in that parameter to a degree, then changing from there to another point so that the sound is perceived as having two sections

imagine another sound with three sections, four, etc.

Crossfades

for anyone

imagine a series of sustaining sounds overlapping from one to the next, with each next sound increasing in volume as the previous one decreases, such that the total volume remains consistent

Delays

for anyone

imagine a single sound

imagine the sound repeated after some amount of time

imagine the sound repeated twice, three times, etc., after some period of time

continue increasing the number of repetitions and/or time interval

Saturation

for anyone

imagine a single sound

imagine two simultaneous sounds, then three, four, etc.

continue to imagine additional sounds until you are no longer able to perceive each individually

Simplification

for anyone

imagine a complex sound

imagine a simplification of the sound by any means

Off Center

for anyone

imagine two simultaneous instances of a sustaining sound, both in the middle range of the same parameter

over the course of each sound, gradually imagine each moving from the middle-ground to opposite extremities of the parameter you've chosen

Sections

for anyone

imagine a static sound sustaining for a lengthy period of time

imagine the same duration of silence

imagine a mass of sounds lasting the same amount of time

imagine the same sections (static sound, silence, sound mass) repeatedly, each time decreasing their duration until they are no longer perceived as individual sections but members of a rhythmic group

gradually increase the section length until returning to the initial duration

Ranges

for anyone

choose a parameter of sound

imagine a series of sounds gradually changing over time with respect to the chosen parameter such that the range of available options for each sound progresses from one extremity of the parameter to the other, although each individual sound may fall anywhere within the range available for the parameter when the sound occurs

imagine the same process in reverse, gradually changing back to the initial parametric extremity

Odds

for anyone

imagine several simultaneous sounds, one of which differing from the rest

imagine a series of sequential sounds, one of which differing from the rest

Attacks I

for anyone

imagine a sound with an extremely abrupt attack

imagine the same sound with an extremely subtle attack

imagine the sound with varying degrees of attack characteristics

Attacks II

for anyone

imagine a sustaining sound, coming from inaudibility to a point of maximum volume then ending abruptly

imagine the same sound beginning at maximum volume then decaying to nothing over the same duration

Attacks III

for anyone

imagine two simultaneous sounds decaying at different rates

Accent

for anyone

imagine several low volume sounds in sequence

imagine a sound distinguishing itself in some way from the others in the sequence via a significant increase in volume

imagine the same process with some parameter other than volume and/or with simultaneous as opposed to sequential sounds

Negative Accent

for anyone

imagine several high volume sounds in sequence

imagine a sound distinguishing itself in some way from the others in the sequence via a significant decrease in volume

imagine the same process with some parameter other than volume and/or with simultaneous as opposed to sequential sounds

Sustenance

for anyone

imagine a sound, unchanging in all parameters, sustaining as long as possible

Durations I

for anyone

imagine the shortest sound possible to perceive

imagine a sound over a much longer duration exhibiting some of the same characteristics

Durations II

for anyone

imagine the shortest sound possible to perceive that exhibits some significant change over time

imagine a similar changing sound occurring over a much longer duration

Durations III

for anyone

imagine the longest sustaining sound for which you are able to maintain a clear focus

with as little pause as possible, imagine the same sound, slightly shorter

again with the least pause between sounds, continue to shorten the length of the sound until no shorter duration can be perceived

Unison

for anyone

imagine a single pitched sound

imagine another simultaneous sound with the same pitch but differing in timbre

continue to add sounds of varying timbre until you are no longer able to perceive each individually, but only a single chorused sound

Counterpoint I

for anyone

imagine a series of sounds implying no particular rhythmic structure or pulse

simultaneously imagine another series in which sounds follow from one to the next at the same interval of time, creating a motoric rhythm

Counterpoint II

for anyone

imagine a series of sounds, all different from one another

simultaneously imagine the same series in reverse

.

Counterpoint III

for anyone

imagine a sequence of sounds

imagine the same sequence again, with a faster version of itself occurring during the original

Pedals I

for anyone

simultaneously imagine a series of changing sounds and a single sustaining sound

Pedals II

for anyone

imagine a series of sounds alternating between one that remains the same in a particular parameter and one that changes

Pedals III

for anyone

imagine a sound changing in any parameter from one point to another, then returning to its initial state

continue this process, each time increasing the amount of change from the initial state of the sound, returning always to the same point

Emphasis

for anyone

imagine a sequence of multiple sounds repeated several times

change the sound or sounds emphasized within each repetition

Deemphasis

for anyone

imagine a group of sequential sounds, one of which is emphasized in some way

continue to imagine the same series of sounds, each time decreasing the emphasis of the member you have chosen until its prominence is lost and it is perceived as equal to any other group member

To and From

for anyone coming or going

imagine a number of successive sounds which lead up to the last sound as a perceived point of arrival

imagine the same number of sounds, perceived as leading away from or subordinate to the first

Fuse

for anyone

imagine two sustaining sounds, one beginning slightly before the other

*attempting to maintain individual focus on each sound, imagine each beginning anew should
they at any point be perceived as a single composite timbre*

Mix

for anyone

imagine several sounds simultaneously

vary the volume of each in several ways, independent of one another

Contours

for anyone, or any group

imagine a sound, changing in some way over a period of time

imagine a group of sounds changing in the same way

Convergence

for anyone

imagine a sound gradually changing timbre until it is perceived as a different sound, or imagine a repeating sound gradually changing timbre with each occurrence until it is no longer perceived as a repetition, but a new sound

Pickup

for anyone

imagine a briefly sustaining sound preceded by a shorter sound such that the first, shorter sound is perceived as subordinate

continue to imagine the same two sounds, each time slightly increasing the duration of the first sound until it is eventually perceived as primary

Inclusion

for anyone

imagine a single sound

imagine the same sound within a larger group of contrasting sounds

Extraction

for anyone

imagine a group of contrasting sounds

imagine any of the individual sounds contained in the group in isolation

Fractal Piece

for anyone

imagine a series of sounds, each of which changes in some way over time

imagine a similar change across the group of sounds as a whole

Framing

for anyone

imagine a brief sound preceded and followed by lengthy silence

alternately, imagine the same sound preceding and following silence

Click

for anyone

imagine a pitched sound, sustaining for a moderate period of time

imagine the same pitched sound again repeatedly, each time decreasing in duration until the sound is no longer perceived as having pitch

repeat the process with various mid-range, low and high pitches

Truncation

for anyone

imagine a sound of moderate duration, evolving over time

imagine the same sound abruptly beginning already underway, skipping the previously imagined initial portion only, ending as before

imagine the same sound with its initial beginning, abruptly ending prior to its previous conclusion

imagine the sound beginning and ending abruptly, omitting the initial and final portions

Undulations

for anyone

imagine a sustaining sound

imagine the same sound repeatedly changing at a regular rhythm with respect to some sounding parameter

substitute different sounding parameters while keeping the same pulse

imagine the sound as initially presented

Drift I

for anyone

imagine two repeating sounds beginning exactly the same and gradually moving apart in some parameter

Drift II

for anyone

imagine two sounds, repeating together to articulate a regular rhythmic pulse

*imagine one sound gradually increasing in tempo while the other maintains the previously
established pulse*

*continue until the tempo is extremely fast, then reverse the process until both sounds again
articulate the initial mutual rhythm*

Drift III

for anyone

imagine two instances of the highest possible pitched sound, both sustaining

while one remains the same, imagine a gradual lowering in pitch of the other

Repeats

for anyone

imagine a constant rhythmic pulse articulated by unique, non-recurring sounds, one after another

choose one sound to recur, which may be repeated in succession with itself or preceded and followed by any unique sound or sounds each time it recurs

notice the perceived rhythm of the recurring timbre while the overall rhythmic pulse remains constant

Interspersement

for anyone

imagine a single sound

imagine a different sound

imagine the first sound again, followed by another different sound

continue this process, ensuring that all of the alternating sounds differ from one another in addition to differing from the initial sound

Overlaps

for anyone

imagine two sustaining sounds of the same duration repeating, one beginning midway through the other

Uncovering

for anyone

imagine a mass of several sounds forming a single overall timbre

gradually reduce the number of sounds until a single sound remains

Interchange with Overlap

for anyone

imagine a repeated rhythmic pattern, each time with different sounds

having established this process for some time, imagine the same sounds comprising the previously established rhythmic pattern, then begin to imagine the same sounds, each time in a different rhythmic configuration

Accumulation

for anyone

imagine a sequence of extremely short sounds each spaced apart at a regular time interval to establish a constant rhythmic pulse

without changing the interval between the start of each sound, gradually imagine a longer duration for each, even as the end time of one overlaps with the start time of the next

continue to the point of maximum saturation

Departure Points

for anyone

imagine two simultaneous sustaining sounds, beginning exactly the same and each gradually changing in a different way

Midpoints

for anyone

imagine two similar sounds, different in some parameter

imagine another similar sound splitting the difference in this aspect

Boundaries

for anyone (within limits, of course)

imagine a sound erratically changing in some aspect within a predetermined range

Plateau

for anyone

imagine a sustaining sound progressing toward a point, then sustaining unchanged once there

Gate

for anyone

imagine a single sound decaying from a point of maximum volume and then abruptly ending upon reaching a moderate volume

Yield

for anyone

imagine a sustaining high volume sound, invariant in timbre

imagine a short low volume sound repeated at a more or less regular time interval

with each instance of the low volume sound, the sustaining high volume sound should stop abruptly and completely, allow the low sound to finish, then immediately resume sustaining

Characteristics

for anyone

imagine several different sounds, all of which share a particular aspect in common

Nestling

for anyone

imagine two sequential sounds perceived as a single pair

*while retaining to the extent possible the relationship between these two sounds, imagine again
with intervening sounds between*

Half and Half

for anyone

imagine a single sound, briefly sustaining

imagine the sound again with an intervening pause in the middle

Reciprocals

for anyone

imagine two simultaneous pitches, one higher than the other, each with a different timbre

to the extent possible, switch the timbre of the lower with that of the higher

Peripherals

for anyone

imagine two simultaneous groups of sounds, one of which is substantially louder than the other

focus on the group of lower volume

Opposite and Other

for anyone

imagine two sequential sounds, each of which exhibits the opposite extremity in some aspect

imagine a sound different from both

Meeting Points

for anyone

imagine two sounds occupying opposite extremities in some parameter, but otherwise the same

imagine a gradual change in one sound while the other remains constant, so that both are eventually identical

repeat the same process, but with the sound that previously remained constant now changing to match the other

repeat the process again so that both sounds change simultaneously, arriving at the same midpoint

Termination

for anyone left

imagine a sustaining sound maintaining a consistent volume

after establishing this sound, imagine a second sound with an immediate decay

imagine both sounds ending simultaneously